Writing Lessons from the Front: Book 2

# Creating Extraordinary Characters

*a simple, practical approach*
*to creating unforgettable characters*

Angela Hunt

Hunt Haven
Press

Visit Angela Hunt's Web site at www.angelahuntbooks.com

ISBN: 061584118X
ISBN-13: 978-0615841182

We cannot judge either of the feelings or of the
character of men with perfect accuracy,
from their actions or their appearance in public;
it is from their careless conversation,
their half-finished sentences, that
we may hope with the greatest probability
of success to discover their real character.

--Maria Edgeworth, Irish novelist

# 1 THE ONE AND ONLY CHAPTER

In light of all the books I've written, people are always asking me to name a favorite. I tell them—truthfully—that I don't have a favorite because I see them all my books as children that I've conceived and birthed, and parents shouldn't pick favorites.

If I'm feeling particularly forthcoming, I tell them—truthfully—that my favorite book is always the one I've just gotten off my desk.

But then I confess something else: I may not have a favorite book, but I do have a favorite character: Sema, the gorilla in *Unspoken*. I love her because she's unique, but most of all I like her because she is loving, protective, funny, sweet, and adorable.

What's not to love?

If you think over the books and movies that have remained with you long after you have turned the last page or left the theater, I'm sure that story's characters made a distinct impression on you. Scarlett O'Hara, Anne Shirley, Pippi Longstalking, James Bond, Sherlock Holmes, Katniss Everdeen . . . we remember these films and books because we fell in love with the *characters*.

## What Makes a Character Memorable?

A character becomes memorable because the author creates him with a boatload of admirable qualities and at least one deep wound.

If you've read *The Plot Skeleton*, the first book in this series of lessons, you know how important it is to spend the first 20 or so percent of your novel developing the protagonist in his *ordinary world*. We meet Scarlett O'Hara in her ordinary world of barbeques and beaus, party dresses and rigid manners. She has half a dozen men on a string and her biggest worry is that Ashley Wilkes, the one man who refuses to remain in her circle of admirers, might marry someone else.

Margaret Mitchell spends eighty-eight pages (12 percent of the story) developing Scarlett's Southern home and heritage, and then war breaks out. The inciting incident sweeps Scarlett away from Tara, the family plantation, and into war-time Atlanta.

The "wound" that Scarlett carries is Ashley's indifference to her declaration of love, but that hurt will pale in comparison to the wounds she suffers in the war: she loses her husband, then her beloved mother and father. Still nursing the superficial hurt Ashley inflicted, she turns a blind eye to the one man who truly loves her, and then she loses him, the daughter she adored, and Melanie Wilkes, the only true friend Scarlett has ever had. With Melanie dead, Scarlett is finally free to love Ashley, but within minutes of realizing this, she sees how foolish she has been. Scarlett has cherished and protected a wound that didn't deserve more than five minutes of her time and energy.

We remember Scarlett because she was a rascal—strong, conniving, loyal (to her own pursuits), bold, brave, charming, creative, and an iconoclast. She was obstinately self-centered and totally focused on her own wants and needs, yet we admired her. Why? Because she was good at what she did. She had the "smallest waist in three counties," she charmed more men than any other woman at the barbeque, and, after the war, she ran a business in Atlanta while most women remained in the home and upheld the social codes of the south. Scarlett did whatever was necessary to survive, and while we may not agree with her decisions, we cannot help but admire the pluck and courage that drove her to meet every challenge head-on.

And who can forget Anne Shirley? Anne is an orphan—many child protagonists bear the wound of the tragic loss of one or both parents—but she goes to live with Marilla and Matthew Cuthbert in the house with the green gables. She is outspoken and brave and loving and imaginative and daring, quick-tempered and delightful. She has flaming red hair, she speaks like a poet, and she loves life with a passion.

And we cannot forget her.

Katniss Everdeen is only fifteen when we first meet her, but from page one of *The Hunger Games* we see that she is brave and resourceful. The family's father has died and the mother still too grief-stricken to rise to the task of caring for her two daughters, so

Katniss has risen to the challenge. Every day she risks her life by entering forbidden territory to hunt squirrels, rabbits, or deer with her bow and arrow. She is self-less; she trades with the government official by agreeing to put her name into the national lottery additional times, thus increasing the risk to her own life. Despite all this, she is self-deprecating, humble, and loving, watching over her little sister, Primrose, like a devoted mother hen.

When I started reading *The Hunger Games*, I cried on page twenty-four . . . and the writer part of my brain marveled that the author, Suzanne Collins, had made me care so much so quickly. How'd she do it? She created a wonderful character with admirable qualities, then let me see those qualities right up front.

So before you do anything else in creating a character, jot down a list of three or four qualities that you admire in a person. Compassion? Fairness? Unfailing cheerfulness? Brilliance in a specific field? Skill at a certain task? An unusual talent?

Choose the qualities you admire, then prepare to inject them into your protagonist.

## Instilling Admirable Qualities

How can you make your protagonist admirable? First, get rid of any notion that your character is going to be ordinary. People don't want to read about ordinary people because we're surrounded by ordinary people every day. We want to read about *extraordinary* people because we read to escape the commonplace.

One of my favorite movies about a writer is *American Dreamer*, starring JoBeth Williams. On the surface, this movie seems to break the "no ordinary people" rule because it's about an ordinary housewife and mother with two little boys and a patronizing husband. But Cathy Palmer has a hidden talent for writing, and when she enters a contest to honor a series of spy novels featuring super-spy Rebecca Ryan, Cathy actually wins . . . and the prize is a trip for two to Paris. Maybe she's not so ordinary after all.

With the help of her little boys (who read the chapter she entered in the contest and loved it), Cathy plans a celebratory dinner to surprise her husband. But instead of celebrating with her, her husband practically pats her on the head and says, "good girl," then he tells her that they simply can't go to Paris. No way.

He is walking up to the house the next day with his golfing buddies, telling them that you've got to know how to keep a woman in her place, but Cathy meets him at the door with suitcases in hand. She worked hard on her entry for that contest, she won, and, by golly, she's going to Paris with or without him. And she does.

In Paris, she savors a bottle of wine in the moonlight from the window in her hotel room, and on her way to the awards banquet the next day she asks the driver to stop so she can take photos of famous landmarks—the Eiffel Tower, Notre Dame Cathedral, etc. When he doesn't give her nearly enough time to even compose her shots, she offers to walk to her awards banquet—after all, it's right around the corner.

But while crossing the street, Cathy is hit by a car. She wakes in a Paris hospital with a peculiar form of amnesia—she believes she is super-spy Rebecca Ryan. And for most of the rest of the movie, she lives fully in her assumed identity, speaking foreign languages, running up bills like a millionaire, flirting outrageously, sprinting through crowds, beating back attackers, and inadvertently foiling a *real* murder plot. Our "ordinary housewife" has turned out to be anything but.

Yet perhaps all the writer did was reveal qualities that had been buried inside Cathy all along. Even before the inciting incident involving the bump on the head, we saw that she was a loving mother, a creative writer, a devoted reader, a faithful wife, a good cook, a thoughtful spouse, and a risk-taker. And when we see her stand up to her condescending, self-centered husband, we see a glimmer of Rebecca Ryan's courageous persona.

Maybe Cathy is more like Rebecca Ryan than she realized.

As you are creating the protagonist for your story, ask yourself:

*What can your character do better than anyone else?

*What makes your character *look* different from everyone else?

*What positive character qualities does your character possess? How can you demonstrate those without having someone tell us about them?

*What negative character qualities does your character possess? (No one is perfect.) How can you hint at those without making us dislike this character?

*Is your character really, really good at his job?

*Can you give your character a good sense of humor?

*Can you put your character into a situation where we feel sorry for him? How can he react to this situation in a positive way? We like people who can handle tough times and keep going. We like characters with self-deprecating humor. We *don't* like characters who whine and complain.

*What is the wound your character received in his past? How has this resulted in a hidden need or character flaw?

Perhaps his first wife died from cancer, and he has always blamed God for not healing her. This has left him completely without faith and cynical in all matters religious. Or perhaps his first wife walked out on him, leaving him distrustful of all women and unwilling to love again.

Remember this: hurt people . . . hurt people, so whenever anyone gets too close to your character's wound, he or she is likely to lash out.

Now that you've done a good job of fleshing out your protagonist, go through the same steps for your antagonist and any other major characters in your story.

### Now That You've Sketched Out A Few Things . . .

Let me confess that I use a shortcut in characterization. It's easy, painless, and I shamelessly recommend this method to all my students.

But before I let you in on the secret, let me tell you what others do.

I have a dear friend who completely immerses herself into her character's personality and journals in that character's voice for weeks. She has a different blank book for each protagonist (she buys a style her character would like), and for her it's like a complete baptism into that character's mind, heart, and voice. That method works for her.

It would drive me crazy because I don't have time for that kind of immersion. I generally take only a week or two, tops, to outline a plot, flesh out my characters, and do any research that needs to be done before beginning a book. I research well enough to get the big picture, and I leave the smaller details until after the first draft. At that point I know what details I'll need to flesh out the scenes, so I don't waste time studying arcane bits of information that I'll never use.

I'm sure you've seen books on characterization that give several blank pages and ask you to jot down everything about a character, including his favorite food, his recurring nightmare, and the names of all his past girlfriends. (I'm exaggerating. A little.)

I am averse to doing work that I don't *have* to do. So I want to know the basics, a little backstory, and enough facts about the broad topic to establish credibility. Why am I so brief? It's not because I'm lazy, it's because I love learning new things. It would be easy for me to get lost in doing research and designing a character; I could spend weeks investigating my settings, photographing the architecture, and interviewing people about the local history.

But all that work would probably end up on the cutting room floor, especially in this age. Ours is a video generation; we expect stories—whether they're in a book or on film—to unwind at a brisk pace. We have no patience with irrelevant backstory, paragraphs of detailed description, or long-winded dialogue. We want the story presented in a simple, elegant, and spare fashion.

So when it came to fashioning characters, I needed a method that would enable me to create real, breathing, fully-fleshed story people in a very short time.

I have the process down to about sixty seconds.

The tool you use for this simple characterization is the Myers-Briggs Personality Indicator.

**How It Works**

I don't want to spend a lot of time talking about personality theory, but let me say that people are wired differently from the moment they are born. We all have a personality that is affected to some degree by the way we are nurtured, but we also have an inborn character that remains basically the same throughout our lives. We can adjust to our environment and we may mellow with age, but all people tend to fall into one of sixteen different personality camps.

Because I'm fascinated with the idea of human personalities, I've taken all kinds of tests and questionnaires and surveys. I've been diagnosed as everything from a Lion to a chlor-mel. But nothing rang true for me until I took one of the personality tests tied to the Myers-Briggs Type Indicator.

If you've never taken a Myers-Briggs test, you can Google one online. Or you can find a free quiz at this link, under the heading "Jung Typology Test:"

http://www.humanmetrics.com/cgi-win/jtypes2.asp

Take the test, or one like it, and your answer will be a group of four letters. I am an INTJ; my husband is an ESFP (clear evidence that opposites attract).

Then you can use an Internet search engine to search for your letter combination: ISTJ, ISFJ, INFJ, INTJ, ISTP, ISFP, INFP, INTP, ESTP, ESFP, ENFP, ENTP, ESTJ, ESFJ, ENFJ, or ENTJ. Several pages will come up, and on those pages you will be able to read all about yourself—your style of communication, your parenting style, what you were like as a child, how you behave as a spouse, how you dress, what sort of home you prefer, the arrangement of your desk, your favorite car, etc. The report may not describe you 100 percent correctly, but it will be pretty close. I'm always amazed at how accurate these results can be.

"All right," you may be thinking, "this is all very interesting, but how does this apply to my writing? How am I supposed to create a fictional character from all this information?"

Easy. Each of the four letters in your label corresponds to a key question. All you have to do is think of a character in your novel, and then answer the four questions with your character in mind.

For the purpose of illustration, let's say that Jesus is a character in your novel. I know he was God incarnate, but he was also fully human, so he had a personality . . . and I think Scripture gives us enough information to help us figure out what type he is. We will also analyze the character of computer expert Penelope Garcia, part of the ensemble cast on the TV show *Criminal Minds*.

1. The first question to ask deals with the first category Myers-Briggs addresses: **Extravert or Introvert?** And the best way to phrase this question is to ask, "Does this character recharge his batteries by going to a party or by going off by himself?" If that doesn't work for you, try "At a party, does this character speak to everyone, including strangers, or does he spend most of his time with a few friends he knows well?"

Jesus traveled from town to town speaking to anyone who would listen, but over and over the writers of the gospels told us that when he was tired, he withdrew. And as we look at his disciples, we see that he had seventy who followed him, then he had the twelve, then he had an inner circle of three: Peter, James, and John. I can imagine that Jesus was like many people I know— they are perfectly at ease speaking before hundreds of people, but when they come off that platform, they retire into the circle of their friends. At a party, they stick with the people they know, because while mingling with strangers is possible for them, it's also exhausting.

I would vote for Introvert in Jesus' case. He spent his days among the people, but he withdrew from them in order to recharge and rest. The people drained him, but people energize an extravert. Penelope Garcia, on the other hand, is probably an extravert. She spends most of her day in a small room surrounded by computer screens, but being with people energizes her and she's not at all intimidated by strangers. She wears clothing designed to call attention to herself and often dyes her hair bright red—she's not exactly shy. But even if she were, Penelope is a clear extravert. She loves being around people and is energized by them.

2. The second question to ask yourself about your character is "Intuitor or Sensor?" If you're not familiar with the way Myers-Briggs uses those terms, ask yourself this: "Does this person take in information through their senses (seeing, hearing, tasting, touching, smelling), and stop there, or do they take in information and then draw on interior feelings to imagine or dream of something else?" Sensors are described as sensible, down-to-earth, and they place a high value on experience and realism. Intuitors, on the other hand, may be described as having their heads in the clouds, lost in fantasy, or imaginative. They prefer fiction over facts, they make decisions based on hunches while the Sensor relies on his experience.

It's a little tricky to evaluate a Jesus character when you realize that he was omniscient and knew everything, but did he base his decisions on his senses or his gut? I'd give the edge to N for Intuitor. Christ saw people not only as they were (sensory information), but as they could and would be. He called Peter a rock when Peter was still trying to find his footing in his faith, and upon meeting Nathaniel Jesus proclaimed, "Now here is a genuine son of Israel—a man of complete integrity" (John 1:47). He could not have realized that though sensory details alone.

Penelope Garcia, however, appears to be a sensor. She lives in a world of hard facts and rarely do we see her going beyond the facts she has collected to imagine how the pieces fit together—that's usually the job of others on her FBI team. She gathers the facts and background information; the profilers put the pieces together. So Penelope gets an S.

3. The third question to ask yourself with your character in

mind is "thinker or feeler?" Now these are not absolute—of course feelers think and thinkers feel. I'm a thinker, but I cry easily and often, so that's no barometer. Both groups experience deep emotions and both groups can make decisions based on logic. But T or F indicates which is the primary emphasis. A man may speak to a group and afterward the Thinkers will say, "His speech was very good—well organized and informative." The Feelers in the audience will say, "I loved his speech! He was so warm and compassionate in his presentation!"

Both groups are telling the truth, but Thinkers and Feelers respond to the same presentation in different ways.

Which was Jesus? Again, this could be tricky, but though Jesus had all knowledge as God, what does Scripture tell us? Over and over, the writers of the gospels go out of their way to write that this all-knowing man was "moved with compassion." It's almost as if they are taking pains to point out how deeply he felt. So I'd give the nod to the F.

Penelope Garcia is brilliant—she even answers the phone with quips like, "Fountain of wisdom, at your service." But despite the fact that she is intelligent, Penelope is primarily a feeler. She can't handle brutal crime scene photos, and she refuses to think about or discuss the details of some particularly heinous crimes. She feels deeply, as do others on the team, but feeling is Penelope's dominant function.

4. The last question to ask yourself regarding your character is "judger or perceiver?" Or, to put it in my personal shorthand, "if you looked at this person's desk, would you see that he's a filer or a piler?"

One day I was in my husband's office while he stepped out. I looked at his cluttered desk and thought I'd help him out by clearing off the dozens of tiny piles of papers and cards and envelopes on his blotter—and then I realized that I couldn't. He knew what was in his piles and I didn't, nor did I know where they were supposed to go.

My desk, on the other hand, does have a few piles, but they're temporary. When I'm done with a project, all those books and papers get neatly filed away where they belong. (I think my blood pressure actually goes up when my desk is messy. I just can't stand it.)

So . . . is your character a planner? Does she create to-do lists?

13

Does she plan her recreation time? Does she sometimes create a list just for the pleasure of scratching something off it? Or is she more spontaneous, a fly-by-the-seat-of-her-pants kind of gal? Is she the sort who would call at a moment's notice and invite you out for coffee . . . or to drive across the state? The first group is made up of judgers; the more spontaneous group is composed of perceivers.

So, what was our Jesus character? He lived before day-timers and smart phone calendars, but when he fed five thousand men plus women and children, he had the people sit down in groups of fifty, then he ordered a proper distribution and collection of the leftovers.

I'm thinking that Jesus was a J, or Judger. He appreciated organization.

So does Penelope Garcia. Yes, despite the fact that she often looks like she encountered a spontaneous whirlwind in her closet, she is very organized, her outlandish outfits have carefully been coordinated, and she undoubtedly has a checklist for every element in her day.

After you've answered the four questions for your character, put them together. Jesus would be INFJ.

A brief synopsis of INFJ personalities would reveal that these folks are

> people whose faith can move mountains. They are happiest when they see their insights helping other people. Many INFJs work so apparently comfortably with others that their associates do not realize they prefer introversion. Because of their clear goals, skill at working with people, and willingness to work hard and long, they may be put in executive positions. They often prefer, however, to work behind the scenes.[i]

Penelope Garcia, on the other hand, would be an ESFJ. A synopsis of her personality type reveals that ESFJs

> love people. They shine at social occasions; they love celebrations in beautiful surroundings with excellent food and drink and warm fellowship. Happiest when they are doing

something nice for someone, they are usually able to say whatever is needed to make everyone feel comfortable. They are likely to choose work that lets them interact with others, and they are most effective when they are given plenty of encouragement and approval. [ii]

You have asked yourself those four questions about a character you are trying to develop, so you should have the four letters that make up his personality type. Google those letters. You'll find several reports, so read a few and see how that information fits with what you need your character to be.

Sometimes you may find that the personality report you get doesn't quite fit the character you have in mind. It may be close, but there's just something a little off. If that's the case, then change one letter—try an S instead of an N. Or try a T instead of an F. Or a J instead of a P.

Read the resulting report from that combination and see if it is a better fit for your character. It's very likely that by trying a different combination of letters, you will find the perfect character sketch online.

**How Character Types Play Out in Story**

Not only will knowing the Myers-Brigg type help you do a quick sketch of your protagonist and other characters, it can also help you with plot development. How?

First, we know that opposites attract. So if you have an INTJ protagonist, give her an ESFP spouse. Their strengths and weaknesses will compliment each other, but you will have a fertile field available for conflict. He, a feeler, won't react to grief in the same way she will because she's a thinker. She will be neat and orderly and he will never remember to put away his socks. He will want her to drop everything and go away for a romantic weekend, but she will resist because she had planned to clean the oven on Saturday afternoon. Worse yet, she will know she's being inflexible, but he should have known her well enough to know she wouldn't want to change her plans at the last minute, and why doesn't he ever exhibit the common courtesy of giving her time to adjust her schedule?

See how it works? Playing character types against one another is natural, simple, and it rings true.

Character type can also influence your character's backstory. Most "feelers" are female, as you might expect, so what happens to the INFP boy? He is sensitive when he's growing up, he abhors violence and roughhousing, and the other kids make fun of him when he cries. So he learns to cover up that tender interior with attitude and a swagger. Now, years later, he finds it hard to dump the old façade to let his wife really understand what's going on in his head and heart . . .

I would do a complete character sketch on each of the major characters in my novel. You don't have to do one on the guard or the doorman, but if any character is going to significantly interact with your protagonist, I'd take the time to flesh him out. You may not use all the information you jot down, but you'll have it if you need it.

**Personality Type is a Tool**
Now that you have your character's personality type, use it for the tool that it is, but don't let it overtake your story. I always read through the personality description and file it away, pulling it out only when I want to double-check something.

Don't let the personality type dominate your story or your story telling. Think of it as the framework upon which your house is built, and remember that a house is far more than its frame. Go ahead and give your character talents, skills, abilities, quirks, and flaws. Just make sure they fit his "personality frame."

For example, I'm an INTJ and I've been an INTJ on every type test I've ever taken. Otto Kroeger and Janet Thuesen, authors of *Type Talk*, say that other likely INTJs include Thomas Edison (inventive genius), Richard Nixon (political genius), and Katharine Hepburn (dramatic genius).[iii] The website www.celebritytypes.com lists Karl Marx, Isaac Newton, Mark Zuckerberg, John Adams, Martin Luther, and Jane Austin as likely INTJs. All these people were marked by confident independence, a key trait of an INTJ, yet they are completely different.

So use the Myers-Briggs to help you define and refine your character, establish his career (unless you want him to be miserable in his work), and determine his parenting style. After that, take him wherever you need him to go, and use his personality type to establish the way he reacts to life.

But don't be a slave to the personality report. It's a tool, not a master plan for your story.

## For Further Reading

The more you read about personality types, the better you will become at understanding what type you need for each character. I've been studying it for so long that I can usually guess a person's type after spending a few hours with them.

Whenever I take a collaboration assignment, I often ask my client to take a quick Myers-Briggs test to help me understand them better. Not only does it help me write their story with more insight, but it helps me understand the best way to approach my client when I'm discussing how the book needs to be written or edited.

If you'd like to have information at your fingertips instead of on the web, you may find the following books helpful.

*Please Understand Me: Character & Temperament Types*, by David Kiersey and Marilyn Bates.

*One of a Kind: Making the Most of Your Child's Uniqueness*, by LaVonne Neff.

*Type Talk: The 16 Personality Types that Determine how We live, Love, and Work*, by Otto Kroeger and Janet M. Thuesen

*The Art of SpeedReading People: Harness the Power of Personality Type and Create What You Want in Business and in Life*, by Paul D. Tieger and Barbara Barron-Tieger

*What Type Am I? Discover Who You Really Are*, by Renee Baron.

A quick search of "Myers-Briggs type indicator" on Amazon.com will bring up dozens of titles with dozens of different applications.

Most books about personality type seem to be found in the business section of the bookstore, probably since most of these titles focus on how to develop and maintain business relationships. But the Myers-Briggs personality indicator can be a valuable tool for writers, as well.

After you have found a personality type that fits the character you have in mind, copy or print the information and store it in your working notebook or computer program. You will want to frequently check back and reread the personality report to make sure your character is still ringing true.

"But," you may be muttering, "sometimes people change. They

do things that might not fit with their type."

You're right about that—to a point. Because what people *do* and what they *are* are two completely different things. More on this later.

## Characters at a Glance—the Notecard

As you are writing, at some point you will need to remind yourself of something about your character—how does he feel about family? What color were his eyes? What year did he graduate from college?

In order to answer these questions quickly, you need to keep all that information at hand. Writers have different methods for keeping this info handy, and I can recommend two: 4 x 6 note cards, or within a computer program.

When I first started writing novels back around 1985, I used notecards. The 4x6 cards gave me lots of room to write, and I could keep them in a rubber-banded stack on my desk. Plus, I could color code them if I wanted—pink for girls, blue for boys, green for plot notes, blue for historical notes. Simple.

Within a few months, I developed a system for what went on that notecard as I began to develop characters and plan my novels. I made sure to make a brief note on the front of each card for these things:

1. Character's full name, followed by his personality type.
2. Date of birth, including the year. Not for astrological reasons, but because birthdays can color our lives. I'm a December baby, and during our first year of marriage my husband made the mistake of bringing me a birthday cake with poinsettias on it.

   If your character was born on the fourth of July, he's going to have strong feelings about that holiday.
3. Character's physical appearance: hair color? Eye color? Short, tall, or medium? Thin, heavy, or average? I am not one for giving much description, and I only mention something unusual—such as a jagged scar across a character's forehead—unless that is going to be significant to the story. If you call attention to it, it had better mean something.
4. Character's dominant personality characteristic—what do

people first notice about him? His awkwardness? His quick smile? His tendency to brag?

5. The character's goal. Some characters may keep this secret, but everyone in your story should want something badly. Every major character should have their own script and personal goals that will, at some point, bring them into conflict with the world and/or with your protagonist.

6. The character's secret: this may not be revealed in the story, but when you get stuck, just have someone slip and spill the beans. Delicious.

7. The character's favorite possession: a toy teddy bear from childhood? A photo album? A Bible? A faded corsage? Whatever it is will speak volumes about your character and may be just the thing to reveal if you need a poignant moment.

8. The character's self-image: we do not always see ourselves as the world sees us. Does this character see himself as a Lothario? As a successful businessman? Is she sixty and yet still thinks of herself as a kittenish bombshell? The greater the gap between the character's self-image and reality, the more potential for conflict . . . and fiction *requires* conflict.

9. Fill the rest of the remaining space on the front of the card by jotting down terms from the character's Myers-Briggs type: Practical, generous, imaginative, orderly—whatever the specific report said.

Now that you've filled out the card front with quick-glance facts, use the back of the note card to write down and personal historical details you might need in the course of the story. Where and when was the character born? When and where did he attend high school? Graduation year? College, when and where?

When and where did he meet his wife? When did they marry? How old were they? When were the children born?

Creating a brief record of these things at the beginning will save you some frustration later. Let's say you're working hard, the writing is flowing, and suddenly your character leads you via flashback to a day when he was a senior in high school. His best girl is beside him in the front seat, he's wearing comfortable Levis, and something is playing on the radio . . .

What's playing? If you know the year he graduated high school (from your notecard), all you have to do is do a quick Google for top ten popular songs in that year. Presto! You'll have your answer in a flash and can immediately drop back into the flow of writing. If you hadn't figured that out beforehand, you'll have to stop and write up a mini-timeline to figure out the when and where . . . trust me, it's easier to do this while you're still developing characters and plot.

I mentioned that I used to use notecards for this sort of thing—I now keep it all on computer, in the same file I use for writing the manuscript.

I used to write with several computer programs open—Excel to keep track of my timeline, Ask Sam to keep track of all my research and notes, and Word to write in. Plus I had notecards on my desk and other information in a notebook.

All that changed a few years ago when I discovered Scrivener. Since then I've discovered that my Scrivener file—just one file for each writing project—can handle all my research, my notes, my manuscript, character sketches *and* character photos, and lots more. Plus, with the click of a single icon I can have the program read my manuscript back to me, allowing me to hear all my repetitions, clunkers, and omitted words.

I didn't intend to include a commercial for Scrivener in this lesson, but I highly recommend it. I use it for every writing project these days, fiction and nonfiction, and only use Word at the last possible moment, when I convert my Scrivener file to a Word file so my editor can read it.

If you're interested in Scrivener, at the time of this writing it can be found at www.literatureandlatte.com, and you can download a PC or Mac version for a free 30-day trial. Enjoy!

**Revealing character**

Once you've outlined your plot skeleton and done character sketches for all your major characters, you're ready to begin writing. And your first task is to create an opening that will reveal the character is his ordinary world, dealing with an interesting and obvious problem, while showing us his hidden need. Oh, and you also ought to demonstrate his admirable qualities so that we care enough about the protagonist that we're willing to spend nonrefundable hours of our finite lifespan with that character.

No small task, is it?
But you can reveal character in several ways:
*through the action
*through the character's thoughts (interior monologue)
*through dialogue
*through the eyes of other characters
*through setting

## Revealing Character Through Action

We discussed the plot issues in book one, *The Plot Skeleton*, so let's focus on the issues of characterization at the beginning of your story. How do you reveal character through actions that don't feel obvious to the reader?

The good news is that plot and characterization work together. At the beginning you are striving to show your protagonist dealing with an obvious problem that can be anything from running late and trying to catch a plane to steadying your pounding heart so that your trembling hands won't jostle the sniper rifle you've aimed at Hitler.

While you write about trying to find a missing shoe or sipping coffee in the snow or chasing the dog who has your boarding pass, you reveal character.

If your protagonist is searching for the missing shoe, how does she try to cajole the toddler who probably hid it? Does she curse at him or turn the search into a game? Whatever she does, we're seeing her character.

If your sniper is sitting on a rooftop in Berlin during a blizzard, if he's sipping lukewarm coffee and has only his thoughts for company, use point of view to tell us what he's thinking. Is he contemplating the end of the war with Hitler's demise? Or is he wondering if he will ever again return to the soft bed and warm wife he left in the early morning hours?

One of my favorite character-revealing openings comes from the movie *Lars and the Real Girl*. The film opens with a wintery shot of what looks like a typical Minnesota farmhouse—two-story white building with a porch, detached garage in back, snow dusting the driveway. The camera turns to the window in the detached garage, then we see Lars, a twenty-something year old man who's wearing a knitted blue scarf around his neck. He is simply standing there, watching the world go by, and then we see the back door open at the big house. A young, pregnant woman comes out, wearing only a short dress and a sweater.

Immediately, Lars ducks out of the window and hides against the wall so the young woman can't see him. Why? Is he afraid of her? We realize that's not the case when she knocks and he comes to the door slowly, but willingly. But he doesn't open the door.

She invites him up to the house for breakfast, and Lars smiles and says he can't come because he has to go to church.

"Then come after church," she says. "Okay?"

The young woman begs, and we realize that she is Lars's sister-in-law, and clearly pregnant. And even while Lars shakes his head and refuses her invitation, he opens the door and takes the knitted scarf from around his neck and gives it to the woman because she's not wearing a coat. He tells her he doesn't want her baby to get sick.

Intent on persuading him to accept her invitation, she continues to beg, then Lars says okay.

"Okay?" she repeats, disbelieving.

Lars nods and steps back into the house, clearly relieved to be ending the conversation. But before he goes, he points to the knitted scarf, smiles, and tells her to "put the whole thing on" because "it's so cold."

So the young woman smiles and goes back to the main house while Lars returns to his garage apartment, slamming the door on the outside world.

The young man has an obvious problem—he's painfully, awkwardly shy. But our hearts break for him because he cares about the young woman, he sacrifices the scarf around his own neck (after all, he wasn't wearing a coat, either), and he cares for her unborn baby. Lars is a churchgoer, a nice guy, and a gentleman, so we fall a little in love with him as we silently urge him to accept her invitation.

But he can't. Because something in his past has made him so shy around people that he would rather remain in his garage apartment than engage with his brother and sister-in-law, the two people who should be closer than anyone else in the world. His hidden need is to overcome that wound in his past so he can be at ease around people, live a full life, and find someone to love.

In the next scene we see Lars at church, where he's helpful to little children and old ladies. One of the older women urges him not to wait too long before finding someone to settle down with, then she gives him a flower and urges him to give it to "someone nice."

Just then a girl his own age walks up and shyly says, "Hello, Lars," and Lars instinctively throws the flower as far away as he can.

This kind, generous young man has a problem, and both his goodness and his problem are demonstrated through his actions.

### Revealing Character through Interior Monologue
In James Collins's novel, *Beginner's Greek*, the protagonist studies a young woman who sits next to him on a plane:

> The young woman sat down. As well as he could, while pretending to idly look around the cabin, Peter studied her. She appeared to be about Peter's age, and she had long reddish blond hair that fell over her shoulders. She wore a thin, white cardigan and blue jeans. What Peter first noticed in her profile was the soft bow of her jaw and how the line turned back at her rounded chin. It reminded Peter of an ideal curve that might be displayed in an old painting manual. His eye traveled back along the jaw, returning to the girl's ear. It was a small ear, beige in color, that appeared almost edible, like a biscuit.[iv]

Nice description, isn't it? We get a fairly good picture of an attractive young girl, but in that paragraph we are getting a far better picture of Peter, the character who is thinking about the girl. (By the way, notice that there are no italics to indicate thought, nor are there any thought attributions like "he mused." Those are not needed when you're using point of view skillfully. Using third person, James Collins has taken us inside Peter's head, so we know we are reading Peter's thoughts. Using italics to indicate thought and switching to first person is an outmoded technique that's simply not necessary. Why switch POV and use a fancy font when you can simply write it out?)

From the paragraph above, we learn a great deal about Peter. What is his education level? Clearly, he's been to college, probably an Ivy League school that offered a classical education. He was more likely to have studied Humanities than engineering. He knows about art. But most notably, he's attracted to this young woman . . . so attracted that he would like to eat her up.

At another point, Peter visits an office and meets a secretary.

> Peter entered and the woman quickly rose to greet him. She was full-figured and in her fifties, with brassy red hair, black eyebrows, and one discolored front tooth. She made every utterance with great enthusiasm.[v]

Notice that the author doesn't give us a string of details. We don't know what she's wearing, nor do we hear any of the exact words she says. Instead, the author chooses the details most likely to give us pertinent information. We read that the woman's red hair is "brassy," so we infer that it came from a cheap home dye job. We read that she's "full-figured" instead of being "svelte," and she has black eyebrows—which do not match the brassy red hair. But the most telling detail of all is the discolored front tooth. With that one element, the author—and Peter, as the point of view character—reveals that this woman most likely did not go to college and this is the best job she can get. She can't afford to get the tooth fixed, and she is not relaxed on the job, so she's making every utterance "with great enthusiasm."

I don't know about you, but I feel sorry for the woman. I'm also a little annoyed with Peter for pointing out her flaws.

**Revealing Character Through Dialogue**
The following is from the first scene of my novel, *The Offering*. I have omitted some of the narrative bits.

> Marilee and I were trying to decide whether we should braid her hair or wear it in pigtails when Gideon thrust his head into the room. Spotting me behind our daughter, he gave me a look of frustrated disbelief. "Don't you have an important appointment this morning?"
> Shock flew through me as I lowered the silky brown strands in my hands. Of course, this

was Monday. At nine I had a tremendously important interview with the Pinellas County school system.

How could I have let time slip away from me on such an important day? Good thing I had a helpful husband.

"Gideon!" I yelled toward the now-empty doorway. "Can you call Mama Isa and tell her I'll be late this morning?"

"Just get going," he yelled, exasperation in his voice. "Your coffee's in the kitchen."

I squeezed Marilee's shoulders. "I'm sorry, sweet girl, but this morning we have to go with something quick."

"Okay. Can I wear it like Princess Leia tomorrow?"

I frowned, trying to place the name. "How does Princess Leia wear her hair?"

"You know." Marilee held her hands out from her ears and spun her index fingers in circles. "She has honey buns on her ears."

I laughed, placing the image—she was talking about the princess in *Star Wars.* "Sure, if you want to have honey buns over your ears, that's what we'll do. We aim to please."

I pulled the long hair from the top of her head into a ponytail, looped an elastic band over it, and tied a bow around the band. Then I kissed the top of her head and took a moment to breathe in the sweet scent of her strawberry shampoo. "Love you," I murmured.

She grinned. "Love you, too."

Twenty minutes later I stood in my closet, wrapped in a towel and dripping on the carpet. What to wear? I had a nice blue skirt, but the waistband had lost its button and I had no idea where I'd put it. The black pantsuit looked expensive and professional, but sand caked my black sandals because I wore them to the beach last weekend.

"Baby girl?"

"In here."

The closet door opened and Gideon grinned at me, a fragrant mug in his hand. "Aren't you ever going to learn how to manage your schedule?"

I grabbed the mug and gulped a mouthful of coffee. "Maybe I like living on the edge."

"And Mama says *I* have a dangerous job." He waggled his brows at the sight of my towel. "Pity you don't have any extra time this morning."

"And too bad you have to get Marilee to school. So off with you, soldier, so I can get my act together."

Chuckling, Gideon lifted his hands in surrender and stepped away from the closet. "Okay, then, I'm heading out. But you're picking up our little bug from school today, right?"

I dropped the blouse I'd been considering. "I'm *what?*"

"Our daughter? You're picking her up this afternoon because I'm leading a training exercise."

For an instant his face went sober and dark, reminding me of the reason he'd been so busy lately. The military had to be planning something, an operation Gideon couldn't even mention to an ordinary civilian like me.

"Sure." My voice lowered to a somber pitch. "I've got it covered."

He nodded, but a hint of uncertainty lingered in his eyes. "Mandy—"

"I've got it, so don't worry." I shooed him out the door. "Tell Marilee I'll see her later."[vi]

No bomb blasts in this opening, just a husband and wife trying to get themselves and their daughter out the door one morning. But what have you learned about Mandy from her dialogue?

First, what kind of mother is she?

Does she have a sense of humor?

What kind of wife is she?

What kind of marriage do she and Gideon share?

In their marriage, do they share responsibilities equally?

Is Mandy exceptionally well-organized, or is she one of those people who is more relaxed about daily activities?

Dialogue, narrative, and interior monologue (thoughts) do work together, of course, but together they can do a great job of revealing character by showing and not telling.

## Revealing Character through the Eyes of Others

Sometimes you can reveal a character by prodding another character to talk about him. You need to be careful, though, lest this technique become too obvious. You don't want his opinion to become an "As-you-know-Bob," as in this example:

Tom and Bob are talking. They have been friends with Charlie for years.

> Leaning over the bench, Tom addressed Bob. "You seen Charlie today?"
>
> Bob nodded. "Saw him over at the clubhouse, standin' at the bar."
>
> "I'm afraid Doug has it in for him." Tom drew a deep breath, then exhaled it through his teeth. "As you know, Charlie has that quick temper. Remember last fall when he decked that caddy? I was afraid Doug had hit his limit then, but what did I know? But this has to be the last straw. "
>
> Bob dipped his head in a slow nod. "Doug's wife always did like them zinnias."
>
> "'Fraid so. And runnin' 'em over was the worst thing Charlie could have done."
>
> Bob picked up the glove that had fallen from the top of his bag. "Looks like our foursome is about to be a threesome."

(In case you're wondering, that excerpt isn't from any published book, but from the top of my head.)

Having two characters tell each other things they already know is illogical and silly. But if you can get rid of the obvious statements ("As you know, Charlie has that quick temper), you can easily have one character reveal character through dialogue with another character. After removing that "as-you-know-Bob" phrase, the above paragraph would do a fine job of telling us that Charlie has a temper and probably a drinking problem, too. (Would you run over a woman's prize zinnias if you were *sober*?)

## Revealing Character Through Setting

An early scene in my book *She Always Wore Red* features a psychiatrist who interviews a private detective in his storefront office. As the detective takes a phone call, the psychiatrist looks around:

> Randolph Harris crosses his leg at the knee and runs his fingers along the trouser leg to reinforce the pleat. The private detective across the desk swivels his chair toward the wall and brings the phone closer to his mouth, employing body language intended to remind his guest that he is not part of the telephone conversation.
>
> Randolph folds his hands and struggles to be patient. He set this appointment for one, canceling two patients in order to drive to this shabby strip mall and meet with Dexter Duggan. He expects a modicum of professionalism in return, but no secretary greeted him at the door, nor did the sandy-haired detective invite him into the inner office until five minutes after the appointed time. When the phone rang at six after, Randolph expected Duggan to ignore the call, but instead the man picked up and launched into a whispered conversation.
>
> Randolph heaves an indiscreet sigh and looks around the office. A laminated map of North Carolina hangs above the desk, with pushpins marking the cities of Raleigh, Charlotte, and Asheville. A bookcase against the paneled wall holds rows of phone books, city names printed on the spines above logos of walking fingers. The second shelf holds camera equipment—several old Nikons, long lenses with capped ends, a battered leather bag, a stainless steel canister with

a black lid. A couple of framed photographs
balance on the lowest shelf, crowded by a pair of
mud-caked boots, a Durham Bulls baseball cap,
and a smudged Panama hat.

He focuses on the photographs: a smiling
boy, probably six or seven, and a bikini-clad
woman standing next to a ski boat.

Oh yes, Dexter Duggan is a class act.[vii]

The paragraphs above serve two functions: not only do they
describe Dexter Duggan and his office, but they also give us a
glimpse into the rigid, judgmental mind of Dr. Randolph Harris.

You can do the same thing by simply closing your eyes and
picturing your character's environment. What does his office or
workspace look like? What's in the trunk of her car? What does she
always have in her purse? What photos does he carry in his wallet?

And when you develop characters, remember this: if you ever
find yourself running short on story, it will be *because you don't know
your characters well enough*. Go back and add more details about your
character's lives so you can know them better. Ask them for their
secrets, and watch them go about their day. Do that often enough,
and you'll have more story than you can handle.

**Deep versus shallow character**
What do you get when you squeeze an orange? You don't
necessarily get orange juice . . . you get whatever's inside the
orange.

In the same way, when life applies pressure and begins to
squeeze your characters, you can get something neither you nor
your character ever expected.

I have never thought of myself as an angry person. I would
have described myself as optimistic and naturally cheerful until I
agreed to take a job teaching high school because another teacher
had been dismissed. I was twenty-two, fresh out of college, and I
was asked to teach eleventh and twelfth grade English, which
meant I had students only a few years younger than me.

I'll never forget the day one senior boy looked me in the eye,
smiled, and said, "We got rid of Mr. Smith in two weeks. We can
get rid of you, too."

In that moment, a geyser of anger erupted inside me. As my

internal organs quivered from the sudden rise in my blood pressure, I thrust out my arm, pointed to the door, and said, "Get out of here. I'm walking you down to the office."

And I did. But as I walked, I wasn't thinking so much about the boy's insubordination, disrespect, and insolent smirk. I was thinking about the sudden eruption of my anger and how I'd never felt anything like that before. Never. And as I held the door open and waited for him to slink into the school office, I wondered if I'd ever be that angry again.

Well. Of course I felt the same eruption when life squeezed me again. What you get when life squeezes is *whatever's inside*. And while I didn't scream or slap anyone or curse a blue streak during those trying times, I think my temper was hot enough to fry an egg.

Agents and editors will tell you that one major problem with beginner's manuscripts is that the protagonists aren't pressured enough. And if a main character is not squeezed hard enough, we're not really going to know him because we're not going to have an opportunity to see what's inside him.

So when you think you've taken your character to his bleakest moment (a la the plot skeleton), move that event up a rib and make the situation worse. And then make it worse again. And then again. Squeeze him until whatever's inside him is running out all over the place and all the world can see exactly what he's made of. *That's* drama.

Our goal as novelists is to torture our characters so that they bleed onto the page. Sorry to use blood and guts metaphors, but it's the truth—you can't be sorry about pushing your characters to their limits and them pushing them again.

As a mature woman with adult children and a grandchild, I can now confess that in my parenting years I found myself saying and doing things I never would have thought myself capable of saying and doing. I have felt emotions I would not have believed I could feel. I have confessed things to my husband that I could not confess in any public arena.

Why? Because life squeezed me harder than I ever thought it would or could. And I am human.

If I am to create authentic fiction, my job as a writer must be to create characters every bit as human and flawed and capable of being squeezed as I am.

In a Donald Maass workshop I attended, I learned a practical character exercise that helps define three areas in which you can squeeze your protagonist.

"Write," he told our group, "something your protagonist would never, ever think."

We thought about our protagonist and the situations in our story, then we wrote.

"Now write something your protagonist would never, ever say." We wrote again.

"Now write something your protagonist would never, ever do." We wrote a third time.

"Now," Don said, "find places in your story where your character can think, say, and do those three things."

Wow.

Remembering that little exercise has kept me writing and my characters reaching. I have let life push them far beyond what they could endure. I have led them to the bleakest moments I could imagine and left them with no hope other than a weakly whispered prayer.

But then help arrived, and along with it, a lesson.

## Creating the Test of Character

How do you squeeze your protagonist so that deep character comes out? It's easy to squeeze him in the latter part of the story because you've probably arranged a series of complications that put him in increasing jeopardy or a time of testing.

You can also apply pressure during the course of the story. The nineteen-seventies brought us a rash of disaster movies featuring ensemble casts: *The Towering Inferno, The Poseidon Adventure, Airport,* and *Earthquake.* Then came the natural disaster movies like *Jaws, Frogs, Piranha,* and *Grizzly,* just to name a few. What did these films have in common? They took an ensemble cast and stripped away the outer character under pressure (from fire, earthquake, bears or frogs), and revealed what lay underneath. The viewers were able to see the politician for what he really was, the agnostic priest who reluctantly returned to God, the fat lady who saved the day, and the sullen loser who tossed aside his enameled mask of not caring to reveal the courage and goodness that lay beneath it. Part of the pleasure for moviegoers was trying to figure out who would survive and who would fall victim to the flames or the killer fish, but viewers found the most pleasure in seeing the characters' facades ripped away like skin from an onion.

But what if you want to squeeze your protagonist at the *beginning* of the story? What if your story is to be about a man who discovers a terrible truth about himself and then has to live with the knowledge of that truth?

Suppose on his way home from work your protagonist comes upon a school bus which has just slid into a retention pond. He jumps out of his car and races toward the bus, then begins yanking children out. The bus is sitting nose down on a shallow ledge, and the remaining children are clustered at the back of the bus, where an air bubble is keeping them alive.

As he swims into the bus, he realizes that gravity is drawing the bus toward the deep part of the lake. The vehicle shudders, and he realizes that he only has time to get two more children.

He surfaces in the air bubble and sees three children gasping for breath—two white, one black.

Or two boys, one girl.

Or two sighted, one blind.

Or two strangers and the son of the man who is making him miserable at work.

With only ten seconds in which to think, which two children does he grab? Your answer—his decision—will speak volumes about his deep character.

And with his decision he will learn things about himself that he hadn't realized before. How does he, an upstanding man in the community, deal with the knowledge of what he has learned? Maybe he grabbed the two white kids because they were closest, and in the aftermath and resulting publicity, he is accused of racism. Does he doubt himself?

If he abandoned the girl, does that mean he values boys more? How does he explain this to his three daughters?

If he grabs the two sighted kids, how can he face the mother of the blind boy, especially after she accuses him of not valuing her son's life?

And if he abandons the son of his rival at work, can he convince himself that he didn't do so purposely? Sometimes we don't know ourselves as well as we think we do.

No matter who he choses, perhaps he feels that his religious beliefs required him to sacrifice himself for those children. Did he show a lack of faith by not diving into the bus yet another time?

Couldn't God have worked a miracle? Maybe he was supposed to give his life that day, and he missed his opportunity to be a hero.

Your job is to construct situations like the one above—something that will test your protagonist and then make him deal with his decisions. If he's conflicted, so much the better, because fiction is fueled by conflict.

This situation you create should test your protagonist's core beliefs, his self-worth, his self-image, and all he holds dear. His decisions may test his family and his marriage. He may lose his job. He may put his life at risk.

But that's a story worth reading.

## Every Protagonist Needs an Antagonist

If no one ever stood in the way of your protagonist, if he accomplished every goal with no interference or difficulty, you'd have a pretty dull story. Your protagonist needs challenges to stretch and change him throughout his story journey, and that's the role of the antagonist.

Do not confuse *antagonist* with *villain*—they are two different roles, and we'll discuss villains in a moment. An antagonist is simply someone who stands in the way of your protagonist throughout the book or at any point in the book.

In my Fairlawn series, in which Jennifer Graham inherits a funeral home in Florida, her mother, Joella, wants Jennifer to sell the funeral home and remain in Virginia where Joella lives. Her reasons are admittedly selfish—she wants to be close to her daughter and her two grandsons.

But Jennifer can't sell the funeral home, and she begins to consider keeping the place open and learning the mortuary trade. The more Jennifer thinks about the idea, the more antagonistic Joella becomes. She doesn't stop loving her daughter, but she does begin to act more and more often as an antagonist, constantly point out reasons why Jennifer should not remain in Florida. By the end of the first book, however, Joella has accepted Jennifer's decision to remain in Mt. Dora, so she is an antagonist no more . . . until book two, when she finds another reason to stand in the way of Jennifer's plans.

So in one scene your antagonist may be the protagonist's loving mother, and in another scene the antagonist is a stubborn real estate agent. The role is up for grabs, and anyone who stands in your protagonist's way can try it on for a scene or two or three.

The role of villain, on the other hand, is more permanent. All villains are antagonists, but not all antagonists are villains. Many books, in fact, have no villains at all.

But if you're writing a mystery or a thriller, there's bound to be a villain, and he will spend the entire book trying to escape, outwit, outrun, and outsmart your protagonist.

This is a good place to ask if you clearly understand the difference between a mystery and a thriller—my experience reveals that most people don't. Both types of book fall until the "suspense" genre, but the two types of book are completely different.

A mystery is a mental puzzle and the reader is in a race against the detective to solve the crime. Both reader and detective are given the same clues at the same time, and a third party usually acts as the narrator, revealing clues to the reader as the detective sees, smells, hears, feels, and/or tastes them. For this reason, it's tricky to write a mystery in first person, because the reader would have access to the detective's reasoning, thus spoiling the reader's fun.

The reader is unaware of the criminal's identity throughout the book, and all is revealed at the end of the story when the detective unmasks the evildoer.

A thriller, on the other hand, isn't a contest. We often know who the murderer or criminal is because we may spend several scenes or chapters in his point of view. We may not know his name, but we know how he operates, what he's thinking, and who his next victim is.

We also know who the protagonist is, though he may not be a professional detective. He may be a lawyer, a writer, or the neighbor next door. But he suspects that something evil is occurring, and he begins to investigate. The villain becomes aware of the protagonist's snooping, and he begins to leave taunting clues for the police and the protagonist. He has more resources and seems to have the upper hand throughout the story, so the protagonist usually seems to have little or no chance of defeating this foe. The reader watches this cat-and-mouse game as the pursuer and the pursued inch closer and closer to each other. At some point the criminal may threaten someone close to the law-abiding protagonist—he may snatch his wife, his child, or his lover. The stakes rise ever higher as the good guy risks everything in order to save those he loves and defeat the man or woman who taunts him.

We wait for the inevitable confrontation, and when it comes, for at least a moment it appears that the villain will win. The protagonist has his bleakest moment, receives help from some unexpected source, and then he wins the battle . . . or at least escapes with his life, having surprised the villain with his courage and resourcefulness. The villain often dies, usually in a gruesome fashion, and the protagonist limps away with his loved ones, scarred but ultimately victorious.

(Of course, this pattern is not without its exceptions, and occasionally the villain does win. But the exceptions are rare.)

See the difference? A mystery is a mental puzzle, a race in which the reader sees if he can figure out the crime along with or before the famous detective. A thriller is a race to an inevitable confrontation between a law-abiding man or woman and a criminal.

## The Anti-hero

Perhaps it's a sign of our times, but anti-heros seem to be more and more popular. Don Draper of AMC's original program *Mad Men* is an advertising executive on New York's Madison Avenue. He's also a liar, a fraud, an adulterer, and a horrible father yet we root for him because he always seems to pull a winning hand out of a lousy deck—and I'm not talking about gambling.

Dexter Morgan, created by novelist Jeff Lindsay, is a cold-blooded, ruthless serial killer who only kills murderers. We root for him because we can support his code, instilled in him by his adoptive father, police officer Harry Morgan, and because we are frustrated when guilty people escape justice. Furthermore, Dexter has a sister, Debra, whom he protects, so we don't believe him when he saw he has no feelings and cannot love. We can see good in Dexter, even though he assures us he has a dangerous "dark passenger." He also works as a blood spatter expert in a police department, so he is working for good even as he plans to kill those who escaped justice and will undoubtedly murder again.

Hannibal Lecter, who terrified us in Thomas Harris's novel *The Silence of the Lambs* and the movie of the same name, now has his own television show.

If you are creating a dark hero, an anti-hero, be sure to give him qualities that allow us to support him. Just as every super-hero has his weakness (Superman and kryptonite, for instance), every dark hero must have some admirable quality or talent or hidden virtue. Otherwise, we'll struggle to find any reason to stick around.

## Why is Your Villain in the Story?

While you're forming your characters, you should do a complete plot skeleton for your villain. You may not need to finish it to the point of the resolution—because your hero should overpower the villain—but your villain has to have a valid reason for being in the story other than simply being someone who antagonizes your protagonist.

I've heard screenwriting expert Michael Hauge say that many romances fail because there's no real reason for couples in romantic comedies to fall in love other than the fact that the script calls for it. Maybe they have nothing in common, maybe the cute hijinks of the movie take up so much time that we never see their true personalities unfolding. Sometimes Tom Hanks and Meg Ryan fall in love just because they're the only two single people in the film—or so it seems, anyway.

For a romantic movie or novel to work, the hero and heroine should have personalities that will mesh (and your Myers-Briggs report will help you determine if that's true). They should have *some* common interests, and they should be compatible.

In the same way, a villain should have a real reason for focusing on your protagonist and choosing to make his life miserable. Is he the president of the company that fired the villain five years before? Did the protagonist's father kill the villain's son in a hit-and-run and get away without serving jail time? Did the protagonist do something to injure the villain or someone in his family in a former job?

Make sure there's a good reason for the villain to hate your protagonist. Otherwise, the obsession doesn't ring true.

Also, remember that the villain's or criminal's crime will make perfect sense to him—he may even believe that he's doing a good thing. The Nazis who ran the prison camps in World War II had been told that Jews were a sub-human species that did not deserve to live. Millions of women have been told that unborn babies are not fully human and do not feel pain. Some people believe that robbing banks is perfectly justifiable because the banks are insured, so "no one really gets hurt." People cheat on their income taxes and justify their actions by saying that the government wastes so much money, it's better to keep it in our own pockets.

On the reality television show *Bait Car*, police officers leave a nice car parked on the street with the keys and a tiny camera inside. While the camera films everything, people jump into the car and prepare to take off, but many of them repeat a common refrain: "Whoever was stupid enough to leave the keys in the car *deserves* to have his car stolen."

See what I mean? We twist language in some cases and logic in others, but people have an extraordinary willingness to justify their behavior. So if you're writing a villain or just a simple antagonist, give him a good reason—from his perspective—for doing whatever he's doing.

### How Many Characters Belong in Your Story?

As few as possible. Readers want to connect emotionally with your story people, and the more characters you involve, the less your reader will bond with them. Sad but true.

Can you have more than one protagonist? Sure, but you're still going to dilute that reader-character bond somewhat. I wrote a story, *The Face*, about a girl and her aunt. They were co-protagonists until . . . well, I don't want to give away the ending.

But in a surprising number of two-protagonist stories (*A Tale of Two Cities*, *The Face*, *A Thousand Splendid Suns*), one of the characters dies so the surviving character can take lessons learned and live a better life. Doing that seems to actually blend the two protagonist-reader bonds so that the reader is focused on only one character at the end of the story. It's a method that works very well.

Three protagonists? In *The Fine Art of Insincerity* I wrote of three sisters. Each sister had her own plot skeleton and followed it to the end of the story, but I made the elder sister the protagonist. The book began and ended with Ginger, and I'm sure the reader bonded primarily with her, though I've received several emails from readers who saw themselves in one of the other sisters.

The more major characters you have, the less your reader will bond with them. You can count on that.

What about point-of-view (POV) characters? Perhaps you have only one protagonist, but there are scenes you need to recount and the protagonist isn't anywhere around. So you need another point of view character, someone who can be in the scene and report it to the reader . . .

This happens all the time, and of course you can use another character to relate what happened.

But if this character is never used again in the entire story, the reader might find it odd to be hearing from him in one scene. There are no hard and fast rules here—you can do as you think best, though your editor might disagree with your decision—but ask yourself if that scene might be rendered as well or better with the breathless participant reporting back to the protagonist.

Example: Michael Jones is a British soldier in the Revolutionary War. He witnesses the murder of a young woman who is engaged to Thomas Oxford (who happens to be your protagonist).

You could write the scene as it happens in story time, from Michael's point of view. But if Michael is never used again as a POV character, it might be better to have a breathless Michael burst into Thomas's tent and report what he has seen.

In fact, I *know* it would be better to have Michael report it to Thomas so the reader can read it from Thomas's point of view. The reader is interested in *Thomas*, not Michael, and they have invested a lot of emotional energy into the romantic relationship between Helen, the young woman, and Thomas. Helen meant next to nothing to Michael, so while the emotional effect of witnessing her murder would upset Michael, the emotional effect upon Thomas would be far greater.

So have the young Michael report to Thomas, and let us be in Thomas's head as he hears the news, and let us see him break down and mourn.

(Or, if he's a scoundrel, let us see him *pretend* to break down and weep while he's privately rejoicing that the man he paid to kill off his fiancé was successful.)

So before you add in extra POV characters, ask yourself if you can find a better way. Most of the time, you can.

### In Conclusion
So there you have it. A lesson on characterization, including bad guys and good guys, plus some tips to cut down on the time you spend staring out the window.

Next up: a lesson in point of view, one of the most common problems for new writers, and how point of view can help you deepen characterization even further.

Until we meet again on the page, create some extraordinary characters and sketch out their plot skeletons. Then create a few characters we will never forget.

Thank you for purchasing this book in **Writing Lessons from the Front.** If you find any typos in this book, please write and let us know: hunthaven@gmail.com.

We would also appreciate it if you would be kind enough to leave a review of this book on Amazon. Thank you!

**Writing Lessons from the Front:**

1. **The Plot Skeleton**
2. **Creating Extraordinary Characters**
3. **Point of View**
4. **Tracking Down the Weasel Words**
5. **Evoking Emotion**
6. **Write that Book: Process and Planning**

## ABOUT THE AUTHOR

Angela Hunt writes for readers who have learned to expect the unexpected from this versatile writer. With over four million copies of her books sold worldwide, she is the best-selling author of more than 120 works ranging from picture books (*The Tale of Three Trees)* to novels and nonfiction.

Now that her two children have reached their twenties, Angie and her husband live in Florida with Very Big Dogs (a direct result of watching *Turner and Hooch* too many times). This affinity for mastiffs has not been without its rewards—one of their dogs was featured on *Live with Regis and Kelly* as the second-largest canine in America. Their dog received this dubious honor after an all-expenses-paid trip to Manhattan for the dog and the Hunts, complete with VIP air travel and a stretch limo in which they toured New York City. Afterward, the dog gave out pawtographs at the airport.

Angela admits to being fascinated by animals, medicine, unexplained phenomena, and "just about everything." Books, she says, have always shaped her life— in the fifth grade she learned how to flirt from reading *Gone with the Wind.*

Her books have won the coveted Christy Award, several Angel Awards from Excellence in Media, and the Gold and Silver Medallions from *Foreword Magazine*'s Book of the Year Award. In 2007, her novel *The Note* was featured as a Christmas movie on the Hallmark channel. She recently completed her doctorate in biblical literature and is now finishing her doctorate in Theology.

When she's not home writing, Angie often travels to teach writing workshops at schools and writers' conferences. And to talk about her dogs, of course. Readers may visit her web site at www.angelahuntbooks.com.

Selected Books by Angela Hunt

*The Offering*
*The Fine Art of Insincerity*
*Five Miles South of Peculiar*
*The Face*
*Let Darkness Come*
*The Elevator*
*The Novelist*
*The Awakening*
*The Truth Teller*
*Unspoken*
*Uncharted*
*The Justice*
*The Canopy*
*The Immortal*
*Doesn't She Look Natural ?*
*She Always Wore Red*
*She's In a Better Place*
*The Pearl*
*The Note*
*The Debt*
*Then Comes Marriage*
*The Shadow Women*
*Dreamers*
*Brothers*
*Journey*
*Roanoke*
*Jamestown*
*Hartford*
*Rehoboth*
*Charles Towne*
*The Proposal*
*The Silver Sword*
*The Golden Cross*
*The Velvet Shadow*
*The Emerald Isle*

# ENDNOTES

[i]LaVonne Neff, *One of a Kind: Making the Most of Your Child's Uniqueness* ( Portland, OR: Multnomah, 1988), p. 179.

[ii]LaVonne Neff, *op.cit.*, p. 163.

[iii] Otto Kroeger and Janet M. Thuesen, Type Talk (New York: Dell Trade, 1988), p. 229-230.

[iv]James Collins, *Beginner's Greek* (New York: Hatchette Book Group, 2008).

[v]James Collins, *op.cit.*

[vi] Angela Hunt, *The Offering* (Nashville: Howard Publishing, 2013), p. 1-3.

[vii]Angela Hunt, *She Always Wore Red* (Wheaton, IL: Tyndale House Publishers, 2008), p. 5-6.

[i] LaVonne Neff, *One of a Kind: Making the Most of Your Child's Uniqueness* ( Portland, OR: Multnomah, 1988), p. 179.
[ii] LaVonne Neff, *op.cit.*, p. 163.
[iii] Otto Kroeger and Janet M. Thuesen, Type Talk (New York: Dell Trade, 1988), p. 229-230.
[iv] James Collins, *Beginner's Greek* (New York: Hatchette Book Group, 2008).
[v] James Collins, *op.cit.*
[vi] Angela Hunt, *The Offering* (Nashville: Howard Publishing, 2013), p. 1-3.
[vii] Angela Hunt, *She Always Wore Red* (Wheaton, IL: Tyndale House Publishers, 2008), p. 5-6.

Made in the USA
San Bernardino, CA
22 July 2014